The World of Insects

# INSECT BODIES

Molly Aloian &
Bobbie Kalman

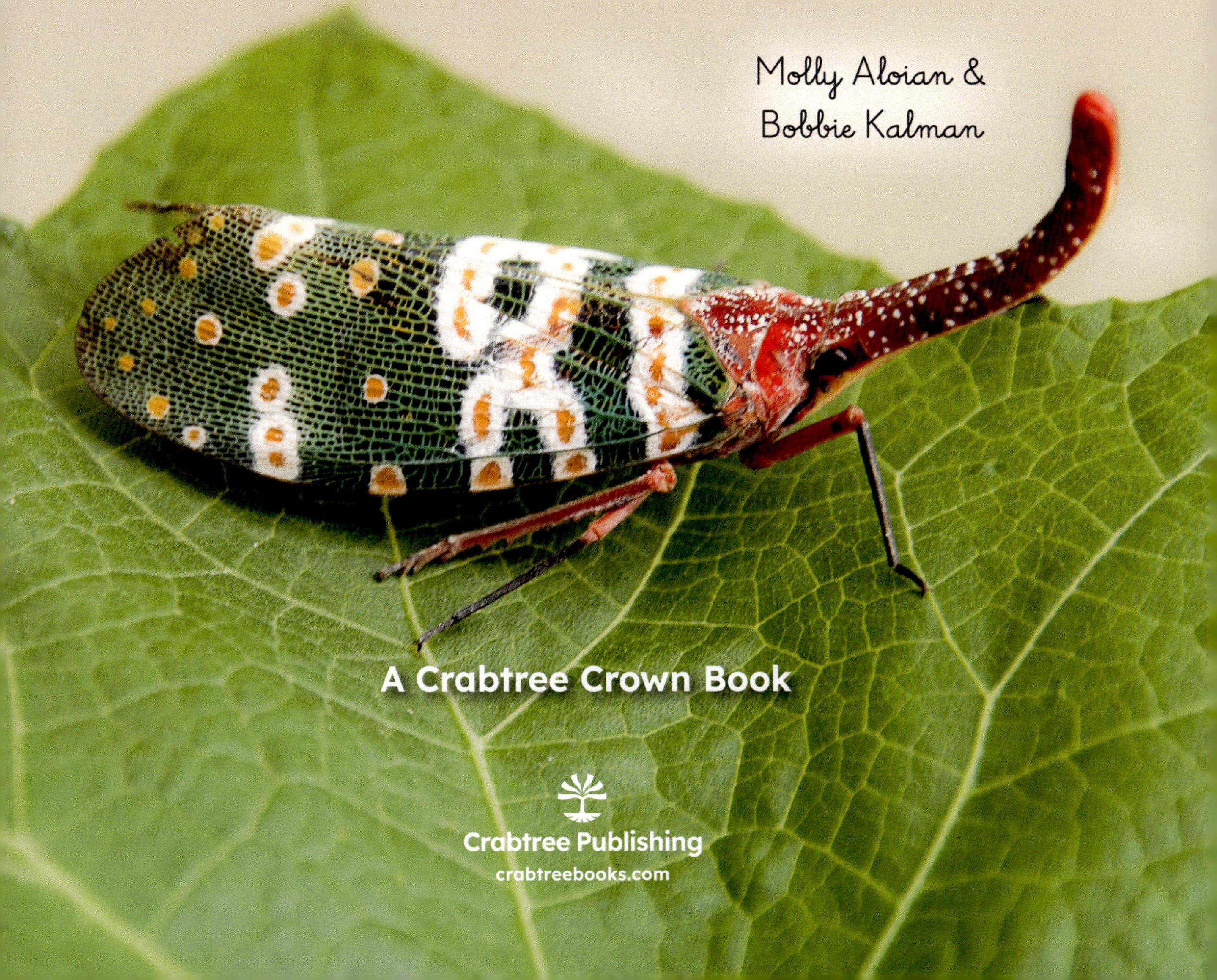

A Crabtree Crown Book

Crabtree Publishing
crabtreebooks.com

# INSECT BODIES

**Editor-in-Chief** Bobbie Kalman

**Writing team** Molly Aloian, Bobbie Kalman

**Editors** Kathryn Smithyman, Kristina Lundblad, Kelley MacAulay

**Consultant** Patricia Loesche, Ph.D., Animal Behavior Program, Department of Psychology, University of Washington

**Design and photo research** Katherine Kantor

**Cover design** Rhea Magaro-Wallace

**Production manager** Candice Campbell

**Images** Shutterstock

**Crabtree Publishing**

crabtreebooks.com 800-387-7650



In Canada: We acknowledge the financial support of the Government of Canada through the Canada Book Fund for our publishing activities.

Printed in the U.S.A./CP022026

Published in Canada
Crabtree Publishing
616 Welland Ave.
St. Catharines, Ontario
L2M 5V6

Published in the United States
Crabtree Publishing
347 Fifth Ave
Suite 1402-145
New York, NY 10016

**Library and Archives Canada Cataloguing in Publication**
Available at the Library and Archives Canada

**Library of Congress Cataloging-in-Publication Data**
Available at the Library of Congress

Hardcover: 978-1-0398-7306-3
Paperback: 978-1-0398-7364-3
Ebook (pdf): 978-1-0398-7414-5
Epub: 978-1-0398-7463-3

# Contents

# So many insects!

**Insects** are animals. There are many kinds of insects. Insects do not all look the same. Some insects are tiny. Others are big. Insects also come in different shapes and colors. Some insects are shown on these pages. How many of these insects do you know?

*fleas*

*ants*

*silverfish*

*ladybug*

## Insects with wings

Many insects have wings. Butterflies and mosquitoes are insects that have wings. Other insects do not have wings. Name all the insects on these pages that have wings.

*dragonfly*

*butterflies*

*wasp*

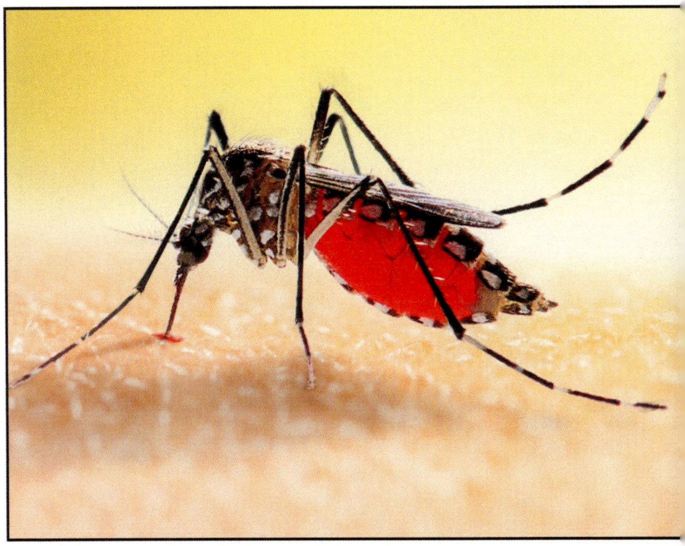

*mosquito*

# Insects are arthropods

Insects belong to a big group of animals called **arthropods**. The bodies of arthropods are made up of small parts called **segments**. The segments are joined together. Look at this blue wasp's leg. The leg is made up of five segments that are joined together.

## Joints that bend

Arthropods have **joints** that bend. A joint is a place where two body parts come together. Your knees and elbows are joints. Many arthropods have joints in their legs and feet, just as you do. They move their legs and feet by bending them at the joints.

### Did you know?

There are more than one million kinds of arthropods on Earth. Crabs, spiders, and lobsters are arthropods, but they are not insects!

# No backbones

Insects are **invertebrates**. Invertebrates are animals that do not have **backbones**. A backbone is a group of bones in the middle of an animal's back. Instead of backbones, insects have hard coverings called **exoskeletons**. Exoskeletons are made of a tough material called **chitin**. Insects make chitin inside their bodies.

## Perfect protection

An insect could not stay alive without an exoskeleton! The exoskeleton protects an insect's body like a suit of armor. It also protects an insect from **predators**. Predators are animals that hunt and eat other animals.

*An exoskeleton covers an insect's whole body. It even covers its legs and head.*

# Three body sections

An insect's body has three main sections—a head, a **thorax**, and an **abdomen**. Each section has important parts.

## The head

The insect's eyes and **mouthparts** are on its head. An insect also has two **antennae** on its head. The insect uses its antennae to feel its way around.

## The thorax

The thorax is the middle section of an insect's body. The insect's legs and wings are attached to the thorax.

## The abdomen

The abdomen is the rear section of an insect's body. It is often an insect's largest body section. The insect's **organs** are inside the abdomen.

## Did you know?

An insect has tiny holes on each side of its thorax and abdomen. The holes are called **spiracles**. The insect takes in air through the spiracles.

*The small black dots on this **larva** are spiracles. A larva is a baby insect.*

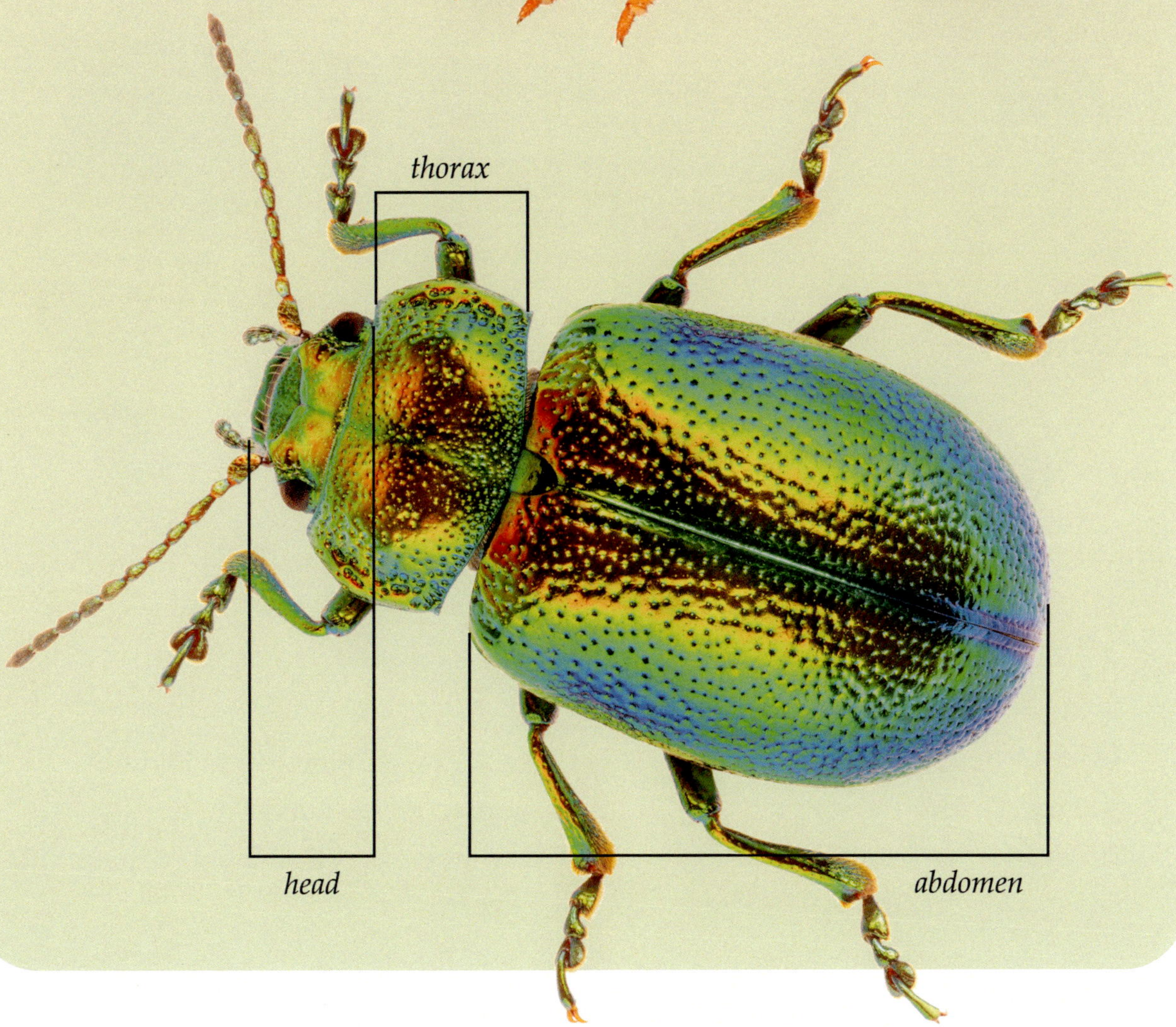

# Insect eyes

Almost all insects have two **compound eyes**. A compound eye is made up of many parts called **facets**. When an insect looks at a flower, each facet of its eyes sees a different part of the flower. The insect's brain then puts the pieces together so the insect can see the whole flower at once.

**Did you know?**

An insect's eyes do not move around the way your eyes move around. Compound eyes bulge out. Having bulging eyes allows an insect to see almost all the way around itself without moving its head.

# Two antennae

Insects have antennae, which help them sense the world around them. They use their antennae as feelers. Different insects have different kinds of antennae. Antennae can be long or short, furry or smooth.

*The longhorned beetle lives in dark places. It has long antennae for feeling its way in the dark.*

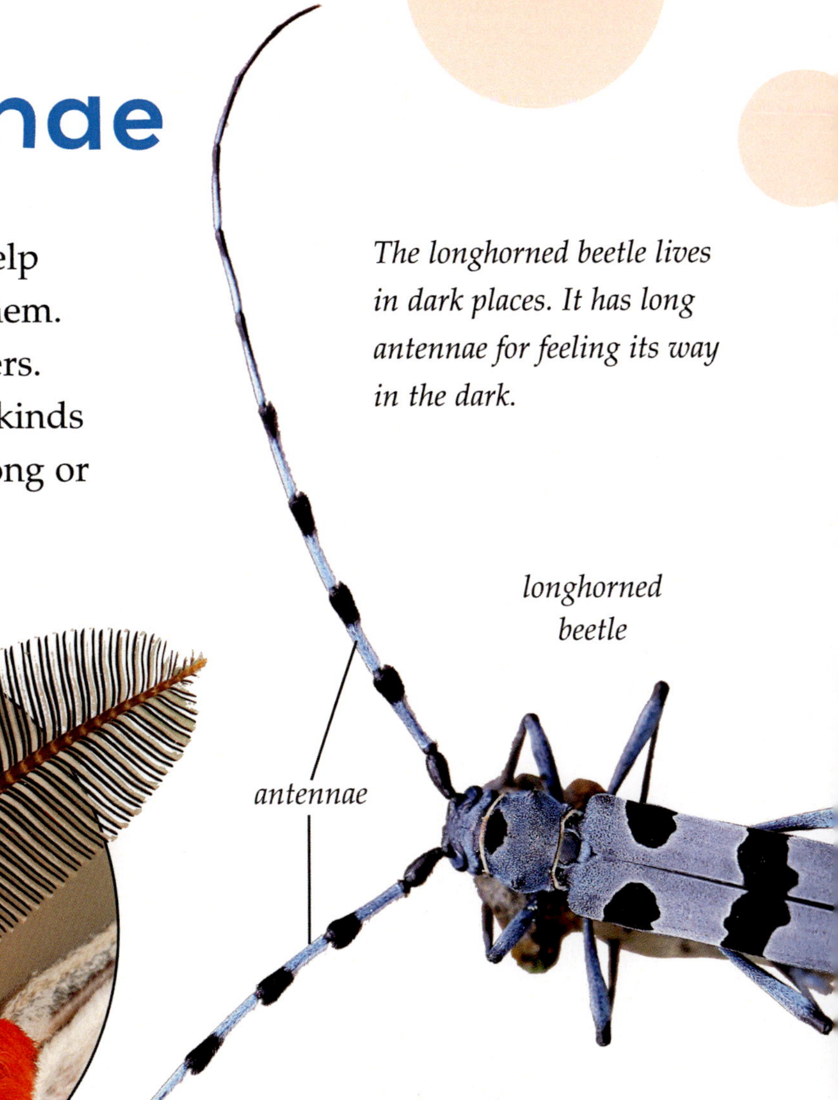

*A moth has long, furry antennae.*

*An ant's antennae have tiny hairs on them.*

*A beetle's antennae are* ***ribbed****, or bumpy.*

# Mouthparts

All insects have mouthparts on their heads. Insects use their mouthparts to grip, cut, crush, or eat their food. Mouthparts can be different sizes and shapes.

*The tiger beetle above has mouthparts for grabbing and chewing its food.*

## Taking a drink

Some insects have long, thin mouthparts that look like straws. A long, thin mouthpart is called a **proboscis**. A proboscis is used to suck up liquid.

*This butterfly is about to use its proboscis to drink* ***nectar*** *from a flower. It will straighten out the proboscis to reach the nectar. After taking a drink, the butterfly will curl up its proboscis again.*

## Did you know?

All bugs are insects, but not all insects are bugs. Bugs are one kind of insect. All bugs have special mouthparts for eating. Their mouthparts **pierce**, or make holes in, their **prey**. Once a bug has pierced its prey, it sucks out the liquid from the prey's body. It sucks the liquid through a long tube on its head. The tube is called a **rostrum**. All bugs have rostrums.

*This shield bug is using its rostrum to feed on a larva.*

# Six legs

All insects have six legs attached to their thoraxes. Some insects have long legs, and other insects have short legs. All insects have legs that bend. Having legs that bend helps insects move quickly from place to place. It also helps flying insects land easily and safely.

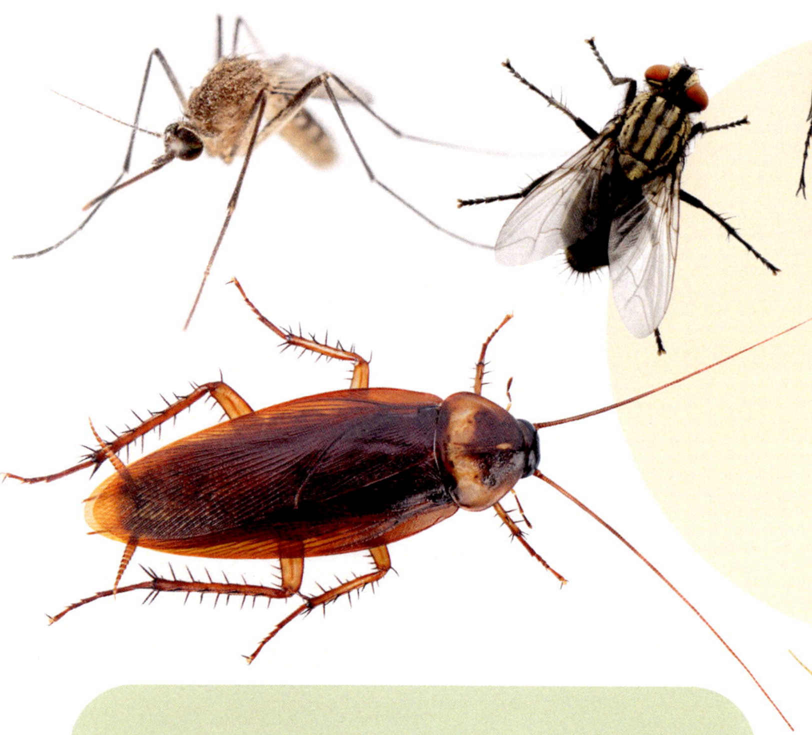

**Did you know?**

An insect runs by moving three legs at a time. It moves one leg on one side of its body and two legs on the other side of its body. The insect then switches sides.

*This water bug is using its hind legs to dive into water.*

## Paddling by

Insects that swim have long **hind legs**. Hind legs are back legs. Swimming insects use their hind legs like paddles to move over the surface of water quickly and easily. They also use their hind legs to dive down into water.

## 1-2-3 jump!

Some insects jump to get away from predators. Like swimming insects, jumping insects also have long, strong hind legs. Having long hind legs gives jumping insects the power to leap away from danger.

*This grasshopper's hind legs are bent. The insect is ready to jump away from danger!*

# Wings for flying

dragonfly

fly

Most insects have wings. Some insects have one pair of wings. Others have two pairs of wings. Insects use their wings to fly. They must flap their wings quickly to stay in the air. Flying helps insects escape from predators. When a predator is nearby, an insect with wings can fly to a safer place. Look at the insects on this page. Which has two pairs of wings—the dragonfly above or the fly on the right?

## Kinds of wings

Insect wings come in many shapes, sizes, and colors. Some insects have brightly colored wings. The butterflies on page 19 have colorful wings. Certain insects have **transparent** wings. You can see through transparent wings. The wings of the dragonfly above are transparent. They are not brightly colored.

## Did you know?

Beetles have two pairs of wings. The front pair are hard wings called **elytra**. The elytra protect the pair of **hind wings**, or back wings. The hind wings fold up under the elytra when a beetle is not flying.

*The thorny phasmid above is a herbivore that eats leaves. It uses its mouthparts to cut and chew the leaves.*

# Insect food

Different insects eat different foods. Some eat plant parts. Others are predators. Predators eat animals, including other insects!

## Plant-eaters

Plant-eating insects are called **herbivores**. Most herbivores do not eat every part of a plant. They eat only certain parts, such as roots, bark, leaves, or stems.

*Most caterpillars, such as the one on the right, are herbivores.*

## Eating animals

Some insects eat animals, such as snails, worms, and even other insects. Insects that eat other animals are called **carnivores**. The fly on the right is a carnivore. Insects that eat both plants and animals are called **omnivores**.

## Insect scavengers

**Scavengers** are animals that eat dead or dying plants and animals. Termites are scavengers. They eat dying or dead trees. The burying beetle on the right is also a scavenger. It eats dead animals.

*The burying beetle is both a carnivore and a scavenger because it eats dead animals.*

# Complete changes

Most insects hatch from eggs. Insects go through many changes as they grow from babies to adults. The changes are called **metamorphosis**. The word "metamorphosis" means "change of **form**," or shape. There are two main kinds of metamorphosis—**complete metamorphosis** and **incomplete metamorphosis**. An insect that goes through complete metamorphosis goes through its changes in four stages: egg, larva, **pupa**, and adult. An insect that goes through incomplete metamorphosis goes through its changes in three stages: egg, **nymph**, and adult.

## Did you know?

As baby insects grow, their exoskeletons do not grow with them. The babies must **molt**, or shed, their exoskeletons and grow new coverings. All baby insects molt to grow. The caterpillar below has just finished molting.

## Big changes!

The ladybug is an insect that goes though complete metamorphosis. Look at the pictures on this page to see how its body changes completely before it becomes an adult insect.

*A female ladybug lays her eggs in a safe place.*

*A larva hatches from each egg. The larva's body looks very different from the body of an adult ladybug. The larva eats and grows bigger each day. As it grows, it molts.*

*The larva makes a hard, protective case around itself. It is now a pupa. When the insect is a pupa, it does not eat or move.*

*An adult ladybug breaks out of its case. The ladybug now has wings and elytra. It can fly from place to place.*

# Growing wings

Shield bugs and dragonflies go through incomplete metamorphosis. Their metamorphosis is called incomplete because these insects do not become pupae before they become adults. When shield bug or dragonfly nymphs hatch, they look like their parents. Nymphs may look like adults, but their bodies are smaller and they do not have wings. The shield bug nymph below does not have wings.

*This young dragonfly has molted several times. Its wings are now starting to form.*

## Getting their wings

Nymphs are often very small when they hatch from their eggs. Their bodies grow bigger each time they molt. Nymphs molt several times. With each molt, their wings form a little more. When their wings are fully formed, the nymphs have changed into adult insects.

*This dragonfly's wings are fully formed. The dragonfly is now an adult.*

# Hiding from predators

Insects have many predators. Birds, frogs, and lizards are some of the animals that eat insects. Insects can run or fly away from predators, but the best way for insects to avoid predators is not to be seen by them at all!

*The color of the toad grasshopper's exoskeleton helps the insect blend in with rocks and leaves.*

## What is camouflage?

**Camouflage** hides insects. Camouflage can be colors, textures, or patterns on an animal's body that hide the animal in its **habitat**, or natural home. Look at these pictures to see the many ways camouflage hides insects.

*The shape and color of this leaf insect's body look just like the leaf on which the insect is sitting. Predators may not see the insect!*

*The bodies and legs of these stick insects look just like the twigs and branches on which the insects live. The stick insect in this photo is hard to spot. Can you find it?*

## Did you know?

Some insects, including the moth on the right, have dark, round markings on their bodies. The markings are called **eyespots**. Eyespots look like the eyes of larger animals, such as owls. They can fool predators. When a predator comes near, this moth opens its wings to show its four eyespots. The eyespots may startle the predator, giving the moth a chance to fly away.

# Insects or not?

Some animals look like insects, but they are not insects! Scorpions, spiders, worms, millipedes, mites, and centipedes are not insects.

Look at each of these animals and guess why they are not insects. Then read the answers to see if you are right!

*scorpion*

***Are spiders and scorpions insects?***
*Scorpions and spiders are not insects. Insects have six legs, but spiders and scorpions have eight legs. What kind of animals are they? Find the answer on the next page!*

*spider*

***Are earthworms insects?*** *Earthworms are not insects. They do not have legs or exoskeletons.*

***Is a millipede an insect?*** *"Milli" means "thousand" and "pede" means "foot." A millipede does not have a thousand feet and legs, but it does have more than six!*

***Is a centipede an insect?*** *"Centipede" means "hundred feet." This animal has fewer than a hundred legs, but it has more than six. It also does not have three body sections.*

***Are mites insects?*** *Mites are not insects. Spiders, scorpions, and mites belong to a group of animals called* ***arachnids****. Arachnids have eight legs.*

# Insect scavenger hunt

There are probably many types of insects living in your back yard. Insects are everywhere! You can learn more about insects by organizing an **insect scavenger hunt** with your family and friends. The more people you get involved, the more fun your insect scavenger hunt will be!

*Be careful not to hurt any insects during your scavenger hunt.*

## Before you begin

Write a list of insects you hope to find in your back yard. Your list should include about ten insects. Give a certain number of points for each insect on your list. Write the number beside the name of the insect. For example, an ant might be worth two points, and a bee might be worth four points.

## The hunt is on!

Hunt for each insect on your list. Make check marks beside the names of the insects you have found. Don't forget to set a time limit! For example, ask people to find all the insects on the list in one hour. When the time is up, have all the "hunters" add up the points beside their check-marked insects. The person with the most points wins the hunt!

*Remind your friends and family to look only for animals with three body sections and six legs. Don't forget that many insects also have wings!*

*Insect scavenger hunt*

*fly* . . . . . . . . . . . . . 1
*ant* . . . . . . . . . . . . . 2
*bee* . . . . . . . . . . . . . 4
*butterfly* . . . . . . . . . 3
*ladybug* . . . . . . . . . 6
*dragonfly* . . . . . . . . 1
*Add your own!*

# Glossary

**Note**: Boldfaced words that are defined in the text may not appear in the glossary.

**arthropod** A big group of animals that have legs with joints that bend and bodies made up of segments

**chitin** A hard substance that makes up an insect's exoskeleton

**exoskeleton** The hard, protective outer covering on an insect's body

**habitat** The natural place where an animal lives

**metamorphosis** The total change in an animal's body from one form to another

**molt** To shed an exoskeleton and grow a new, bigger exoskeleton

**nectar** A sweet liquid that is found in flowers

**nymph** A young insect that does not yet have wings

**organ** A part of an animal's body, such as the heart, which does an important job

**prey** An animal that is eaten by predators

**pupa** The stage between the larva and the adult, which certain insects go through during their complete metamorphosis

# Index